RACISM

© Aladdin Books 1990

Designed and produced by
Aladdin Books Ltd, 28 Percy Street, London W1P 9FF

Design: Andy Wilkinson
Editorial: Catherine Bradley, Elise Bradbury
Picture Research: Emma Krikler
Illustrator: Ron Hayward Associates

A CIP catalogue record for this book is available from the British Library.

The publishers would like to acknowledge that the photographs reproduced within this book have been posed by models or have been obtained from photographic agencies.

Angela Grunsell is an advisory teacher specialising in development education and resources for the primary school age range.

The consultant, Sharon Dillette, is a deputy head of a North London junior school.

The consultant, Pete Sanders, is the head teacher of a North London primary school.

First published in Great Britain in 1990 by
Franklin Watts Ltd, 96 Leonard Street, London EC2A 4RH

ISBN 0 7496 0432 8
Printed in Belgium   All rights reserved

"L-T'S TALK ABOUT"

RACISM

ANGELA GRUNSELL

Gloucester Press
London · New York · Toronto · Sydney

Everyone has a right to respect and justice. Racism means that some people get neither.

4

"Why talk about racism?"

Racist jokes, name-calling and violent racist attacks happen all the time and yet many people try to pretend that racism is not a problem. If you look and listen carefully, you will come across racism every day. Racism means that some people make judgements about you without bothering to find out what you are like. Some people get treated unfairly because of racism. Racism deepens misunderstanding between groups of people who could learn from each other and live together. There are thousands of racist attacks in Britain every year. Many families live in fear because of threats to them and their homes.

This book looks at what racism is, what its effects are and why it is so harmful to everyone. It shows how racism comes out in people's comments. It describes how racism is used by rulers to increase their power and make ordinary people fear each other.

The similarities of all members of the human race are greater than any differences.

6

"What is racism?"

We all belong to one race, the human race. But everyone is different. We are all individuals. You are not the same as your mother or father, brothers or sisters, although you may look like them. Your whole personality and body are all your own. You may look more like some people in your class than others, but that does not mean you are similar to them. Your best friend may have another religion or speak another first language from you.

Racism is the mistaken belief that there are distinct groups, or races, within the human race, with particular characteristics which affect how they behave. People with these ideas think "their" race is better than others. The views of those around them and some books, newspapers and films may have misled them into thinking in this way. Scientists have been unable to discover ways of separating the human race into distinct races.

Racism occurs when you distance yourself from someone else because you think they come from a different place or kind of people. You decide that they do not belong to your group. You do this because of a person's colour or the way they talk or sometimes their religion.

As a result of racism some groups in our society have more power and status than others. Racial discrimination – which means giving houses, jobs or educational opportunities on the grounds of race – is against the law in Britain. But racial abuse happens in many places: on the bus, in the playground, and even in the classroom. Although people can take cases of racial abuse to court, it can be very difficult to prove what exactly happened. However, when someone wins a case of racial discrimination, it shows that people are willing to work for a fairer society.

It takes courage to find out what a person is really like if friends or parents are telling you not to. Michael and Ngugi are in the same class. Michael said, "I don't play with Africans". This is racism. The two boys support the same football team, like the same music, share the same favourite foods. If Michael had asked Ngugi about himself, he would have found this out. They have more in common than Michael and his cousin. But Michael was prejudiced against Ngugi without even speaking to him.

Everyone would think it unfair and ridiculous if only those children wearing the same colour clothes were allowed to play together in the playground.

"What is prejudice?"

Prejudice means deciding in advance what someone is like instead of finding out for yourself. Racially prejudiced people think that because an individual belongs to a group which shares a certain language or accent, skin colour or religion, then they know what that person is like.

They will sometimes say "they're all lazy or stupid" or "you can't trust them". If they do form a friendship with someone who belongs to a group they are prejudiced against, they say, "Well she's different". But they do not allow their experience to change their false or stereotyped views about people in that group.

Many people enjoy being supporters of a team without needing to bully or insult the fans of the other team.

"What is a stereotype?"

A stereotype is a fixed idea about what people are like. For example, advertising uses stereotypes by creating images of "perfect mothers" to sell soap powder. If you get stereotyped by others it can be hard to try out different ways of behaving. You may not get treated seriously if you are known as the class clown. Stereotyping reduces whole groups of people to one characteristic, for example, calling all Scots "mean". Racial stereotyping means that some teachers expect all black children to be athletic. Stereotypes are dangerous because they can limit how you see others and how you see yourself.

> Mae Jamieson is a US astronaut. All children need to be able to see that if they want to become an astronaut, a scientist or a judge, it is possible for them to do it.

"Where did today's racism come from?"

Over the last 500 years European countries sent men to invade the Americas, Africa and Asia. They seized many territories, killed the local peoples and created countries which they ruled as colonies. Europeans grew very rich because cheap food and raw materials for their factories were being produced by slave labour in the colonies. So that ordinary people would accept their actions, European leaders spread stories that the people living in the colonies were primitives and disorganised. Europeans began to look down on unfamiliar religions and ways of life.

This map shows how countries had built up empires by 1914. Today the colonies are independent but they still produce food and raw materials for Europeans.

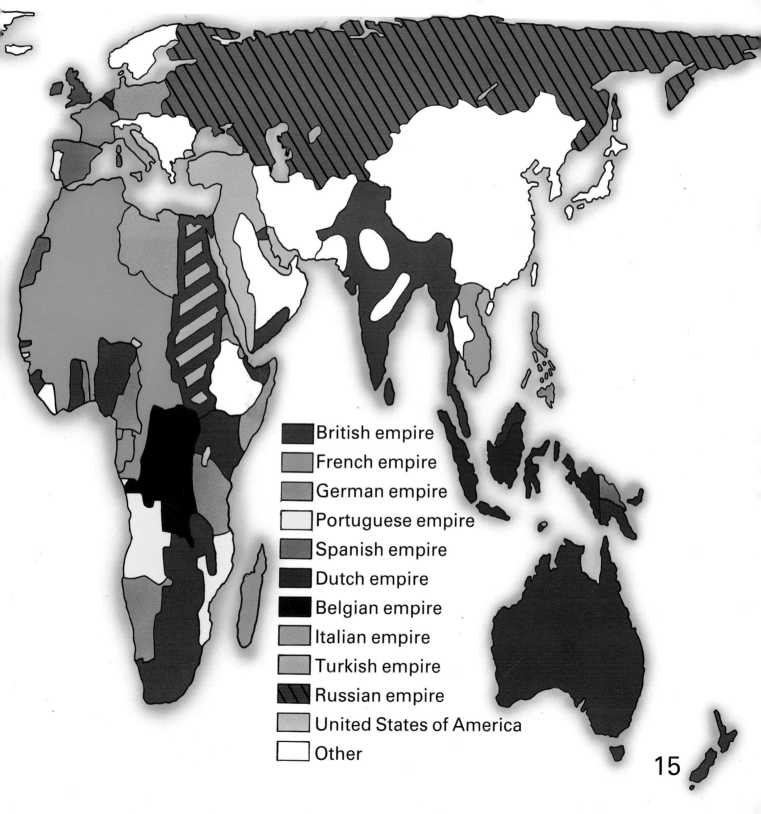

British empire
French empire
German empire
Portuguese empire
Spanish empire
Dutch empire
Belgian empire
Italian empire
Turkish empire
Russian empire
United States of America
Other

15

"How do racist ideas get passed on?"

Babies are not racist. They trust and accept anyone who is loving to them. You are not born with attitudes and prejudices, they are taught and learned. Racist ideas get passed on when people talk to others or write or make pictures. Parents teach children the names to give things. They also teach their own attitudes to them along with the names. A cottage and a mud hut are the same, but the two words conjure up different pictures. Many people would like to live in a thatched cottage without knowing it is made out of mud. Racist ideas can become part of a language.

Pictures can pass on racist ideas by not showing us people in other places as individuals. Tea-pickers often work long hours for low wages.

"Why is there racism today?"

Some people today think that they will benefit from being racist. They may be afraid or jealous of other groups. They may blame difficulties in their own lives on other people. They may have learned from their parents to resent and mistrust people from other groups. They may believe the racist stereotypes and ideas that have been passed on to them. They may be white or black, Jewish, Muslim or Christian. Anybody can be racist. Bullies often use racism as an excuse for violent behaviour.

This boy is an Aborigine living in Australia. He experiences racism today because his people are denied many rights. In the past European settlers took Aborigine land away by force.

19

Nazi Germany occupied much of Europe and millions of Jews were forced into concentration camps and killed. These Jewish women and children are waiting to go to a camp.

"Why is racism so harmful?"

Racism benefits no one. It creates mistrust between people. In some countries, leaders have used resentments between groups to create hatred and suspicion between people. Politicians have used ordinary people's prejudice to get support for their racist ideas and actions.

In the 1930s Hitler and the Nazis in Germany persuaded their followers to blame everything that was wrong in their lives on the Jews – as well as homosexuals and communists. Nazi gangs attacked Jews and destroyed their property. Laws were passed to stop Jewish people owning their own businesses and to prevent them from having the same rights to health care, education and even protection by the police, as other people. Many Jews fled from Germany but some **fought back**. Others were sent to concentration camps and nearly six million of them died. The Nazis were defeated by other countries in 1945.

The release of black leader, Nelson Mandela, after 27 years in prison was brought about by people all over the world who believe that racism and Apartheid are unjust and destructive.

Accepting racist beliefs means hoping that you will benefit from the unjust treatment of other people. Racism means that people are divided against each other instead of learning to live together peacefully.

In South Africa, people of European origin are still holding onto land they took over the last 300 years. There are only 4.5 million whites and 22.3 million blacks. Whites own 87 per cent of the best land while the blacks have only 13 per cent. In South Africa the whites have forced black people to accept an Apartheid (separateness) system. The Apartheid system of laws means that the whites control where black people live and work and even who they can marry. Black children do not get as much money spent on their education as white children.

These laws have kept wealth and power in the hands of white people. Apartheid is based on racist ideas that black and white are different and should live and develop separately because whites are superior. Black South Africans have never given up the hope of getting their land back. They fight for their rights as human beings. Things are changing because millions of black and white people, inside and outside South Africa, believe that Apartheid is evil and wrong and should be changed.

"What about racism in our school?"

When you understand what racism can lead to, you can understand that racist incidents are more than a problem between two or three people. You can begin to see how it brings about hatred, murder and war. Racism means that people from some groups are attacked in their homes and on the street. You may want to do something to make your school a safe place for everyone. Especially if you have been called racist names yourself, you can begin to see that doing it to other people helps to keep the whole system going which has hurt you.

In many schools children and adults work on anti-racist policies. This painting was done by children who worked together on a charter for human rights after studying South Africa.

Changing how things are can start with individuals getting together with others who feel the same way. You have the power to start to challenge racism in your classroom and your school by talking about it with your teacher.

Your teacher may not know what is happening in the playground or the toilets or even in the dinner queue until you tell her or him. You and your friends can talk to your head teacher too. You may need help from parents or other adults. When you have class discussions about racism you begin to find out what is happening to other children and how they feel about it.

Racism is far from being only a black and white issue; there is racism against many groups. For example, in Britain the Irish are still discriminated against. Racism goes back a long way in history and is rooted in our language. So this is something everyone needs to learn about and see clearly. One way of changing attitudes is to find out more about how other people live. You can add to your enjoyment of life by finding out about the languages, religions, cookery, art and music of groups you are not very familiar with. You will meet people who at first sight are not exactly like you. You can use this opportunity to ask them about their lives and talk about your own way of life.

The more you know about other people and they know about you, the less you will be divided by racism. The Chinese celebrate their New Year in many British cities.

"How do I deal with racist insults?"

Any group can become the target of racism. Feeling good about who you are cannot prevent other people from insulting you, but it can help you to deal with it better. You can learn to avoid some confrontations, by acting with dignity and refusing to let other people annoy you. You may need to judge quite carefully the right moment to stand up for yourself and others, and when to get help, or simply leave a situation quickly. Everyone needs to learn ways of surviving. When people get together to take action against unfair treatment, they can change things.

> You do not have to put up with racial discrimination or bullying. If you need help, ask for it and work out the best way of challenging the people who are getting at you.

What can I do?

This book has shown you how racism works both between individuals and in countries. You have learned that prejudice and stereotypes – even through jokes and comments – create and maintain racist ideas. You will never learn to understand yourself or other people if you let yourself be guided by such ideas.

Although the book has talked a lot about black and white, there are many other examples of racism past and present you can find out more about.

You can choose to challenge racism when you come across it in ways that work for you. You can try to be open to everyone you meet and to find out more about what they are really like by listening and talking.

Addresses for further information

ChildLine
Freepost 1111
London N1 0BR
Tel: 0800 1111

Commission for Racial Equality
Elliot House, 10-12 Allington St
London SW1E 5EH
Tel: 071 828 7022

What the words mean

Apartheid is the South African system for keeping groups or races apart and enforcing this with laws.

concentration camp is a prison where people are forced to live and work in very basic conditions.

discrimination occurs when people put others at a disadvantage.

empire is a group of lands which are under the rule of a dominant country.

prejudice is having an opinion or deciding about something or someone without finding out for yourself – you pre-judge.

racism is a belief that there are human groups with particular characteristics. It is used to justify the unfair treatment of others.

stereotype is a false picture which links people from particular groups with certain, usually negative, characteristics.

Index

Photographic Credits:
Cover and pages 4-5, 6-7, 8-9 and 28-29: Marie-Helene Bradley; page 11: Topham Photo Library; page 12: Frank Spooner Pictures; page 16: Rex Features; page 18-19: ICI Corporate Slide Bank; page 20-21: The Institute of Contemporary History and Weiner Library; page 22-23: International Defence and Aid Fund for Southern Africa; page 24-25: taken at Dulwich Hamlets Primary School (by Art and Development Education Project); page 26-27: Network Photographers.

PRINTED IN BELGIUM BY
proost
INTERNATIONAL BOOK PRODUCTION